THE WILD PUPS

THE WILD PUPS
The True Story of a Coyote Family

by Hope Ryden

G. P. Putnam's Sons
New York

At first the pups were a secret. Mama Redlegs did not allow any of the coyotes who lived on Miller Butte to enter the burrow where her babies had been born. And because the tiny brown pups were not yet able to see or hear or even crawl, they could not climb up the long tunnel that led from their underground chamber into the sunshine.

Gray Dog sensed something was up and he watched from afar. He was Redlegs' mate.

Sometimes Gray Dog acted as if he wanted to enter the den to see what was keeping Redlegs below ground all day. But Redlegs blocked his way and made clear by means of coyote body language that she would not let him enter.

Still, whenever Redlegs heard Gray Dog, she would run to meet him with her tail wagging vigorously. At a safe distance from her den she would greet him with kisses and playful taps of her paw.

As soon as their "hellos" were over, Gray Dog's sides would begin to convulse until he managed to bring up all the mice and ground squirrels he had caught and swallowed that morning. Then he would step back and watch Redlegs eat the food he had offered her. He carried food to her in his stomach instead of by mouth because his stomach could hold more. This saved him from having to make many trips.

Redlegs ate quickly and went back to her pups. Gray Dog then trotted off to the marsh to stalk and pounce on more unsuspecting mice and ground squirrels.

Other coyotes, too, lived on Miller Butte and were curious about what was in Redlegs' burrow. Seven adult coyotes belonged to the Miller Butte pack. They were friendly with one another, but they did not allow any strange coyotes to hunt on their territory.

Sometimes all seven gathered to enjoy a good howl. Howling was important to the Miller Butte coyotes. It warned strange coyotes not to trespass on their hunting ground. It helped pack members keep track of one another's whereabouts. It also strengthened their feelings of friendship for one another.

Whenever they came together to howl, they would first show their pleasure and excitement by pushing at one another with their long pointy noses and by wagging their tails. After this greeting, one or another would "strike a note," and instantly all the coyotes would throw back their heads and "sing" until the very rocks and trees echoed with their wild music.

    When the pups were about ten days old, they crawled
out of the dark burrow and into the sunshine. At this early
stage they looked more like ground squirrels than baby coyotes.
Their coats were very dark, their eyes were barely opened,
and their noses were short and stubby.

But Redlegs did not seem to mind that her babies were shapeless, wriggling lumps. She seemed satisfied with everything about them. And now that they were able to be outside their den, she no longer kept Gray Dog away from them. In fact, while he was getting to know them, Redlegs stood to one side and wore a big dog grin.

Over the next few weeks Redlegs behaved in a way that would make a person think she was proud. And, indeed, if she did feel something like that, who could blame her? With every passing day her babies grew more appealing.

Their dark coats
faded to a golden tan.
Their snouts lengthened.
And their ears
stood up on their heads
like little sails.

Even so, being surrounded by a litter of active pups often
tired Redlegs. Sometimes she longed to go off by herself to
hunt mice or to lie beside a quiet stream.

Happily every member of the
Miller Butte pack was ready and
willing to look after the babies
in her absence. Males as well as
females hung about the den just
waiting for a chance to be
with the pups. Here Gray Dog
acts as a baby-sitter.

Every member of the Miller Butte pack brought food to the
pups, too, which had first been chewed and swallowed to make
it more digestible. Whenever a little one felt hungry, all he
had to do was nuzzle the mouth of an adult and the grown
coyote would bring up something for him to eat.

Sometimes two or three coyotes would look after the babies at the same time. Nature had provided the pups with foster parents. Should their real parents be killed, they would surely be taken care of.

Even though the pups were content to be left with any member of the Miller Butte pack, they always acted glad to see their mother again. When they spied her returning from a hunt, they would dash downhill to meet her. She would then nurse them in a standing position. This meant the pups had to get up on their hind legs to reach her breasts. Although this was awkward for them, it allowed Redlegs to keep a watch out for danger.

With so much care and food and loving attention given them,
the pups were free to spend the spring days playing. And they did.

They played the same games dog puppies like. Of course they had no rubber balls or squeaky toys. Instead they played with old bones, their tails . . .

and even clods of earth that fell apart in the middle of
games of tug-o'-war.

Playing was not only fun, it was important. It helped the pups develop strong bodies. It also taught them to get along with one another. Through play the young coyotes formed friendships that could last a lifetime.

And through play the baby coyotes learned to control their bites. This is a most important lesson for coyotes to learn. Nature has provided them with sharp teeth and powerful jaws for obtaining food. During its history, had the coyote used these weapons against its own kind, it would have died out. So after a few battles in which the pups experienced some painful nips they learned to make their bites gentle and not to inflict real pain.

Since the pups would soon have to find their own food, it was important that they begin to practice hunting. At four weeks of age they started to spend part of every day stalking and pouncing on grasshoppers and beetles.

They soon became expert at this, and one day one of the pups surprised himself by catching a real live mouse! With his trophy dangling from his mouth, he proudly strutted before his brothers and sisters until one of them could stand it no longer. In a swift attack the envious brother seized the little hunter's prize.

One day Redlegs signaled the pups to follow her. She had taken them on short trips before, and, like ducks in a line, they always followed her obediently. But on this day the pups could not have suspected how far they would be led. On and on they trailed. Higher and higher they climbed . . .

until at last they came to some thick willows that crowned
the far end of the butte. The pups had been moved to
a new home.

It was a wonderfully safe place for them. The willows provided
them shelter from the rain and a perfect place in which to hide.
In the thick brush they were all but impossible to see.

At the same time they were able to keep watch in every direction.
No enemy could climb the steep slope unnoticed by them.
Redlegs had selected an ideal home for her growing young.

And grow they did. With each
passing week their legs lengthened,
their tails grew bushier, and
their spirits more independent.
And what skillful mousers they
became!

Still much remained for them to
learn from the wise old members of
the pack. And so they continued to
live on top of the butte throughout
the summer and into fall.

And then one day snow fell. What a surprise this gave Redlegs' young (who by now had thick coats and looked quite grown up). Never before had they seen the world look so bright. The cold flakes splashed on their noses, and white drifts rose about their feet. It made some of the pups feel like playing. They could not have suspected that winter means hard times for wild animals. Finding food would now become very difficult. No longer would it be possible for the older coyotes to offer extra food to the young ones. In the months ahead it would be every coyote for himself, and only the strong would survive.

Still the older coyotes would continue to pass on their knowledge.

In the weeks that followed, the young watched how the experienced coyotes hunted mice under the snow. Soon they, too, were alert to the faint sounds of rodents scurrying beneath the swollen drifts. And with growing skill they plunged headfirst into snowbanks to pluck out dinner.

It was a hard way to make a living, though. Sometimes the coyotes would struggle across the blinding snow all day without finding anything to eat. Slogging through deep drifts was tiring work. Whenever they could, the older coyotes walked on surfaces that had frozen solid and would support their weight. Even so, the ice made their feet sore.

To avoid unnecessary walking, the coyotes
watched the sky for ravens who might lead them directly to food.

A raven is a large black bird that eats many of the things coyotes do. Both coyotes and ravens feed on any dead animals they happen to find. When a raven spies a dead deer or elk lying on the ground, he flies about the spot and croaks the news of his discovery to his flock. Many coyotes seem to understand this raven-talk. They head directly for the hovering birds and join them in cleaning up the carcass. Coyotes and ravens are often seen together. When two species serve each other, they are said to have a symbiotic relationship.

As if winter weren't difficult enough for Redlegs' pups, fur trappers added to their problems. In cold weather animals' coats are thick and beautiful, and each winter hundreds of thousands of wild creatures are taken in traps so people can wear their skins.

A coyote who is caught in a leg-hold trap may bite off its paw to escape. Those who cannot free themselves must lie in the same position for days until the trapper returns to kill them. Many freeze or slowly starve. Some are eaten by other animals. Leg-hold traps are cruel devices, and a number of countries have outlawed them. Many people in the United States want to see them outlawed here, too.

Any coyote who has had a near miss with a leg-hold trap
will forever after be extremely wary about what food he eats.
He does not want to spring another baited trap.

So no matter how hungry he may be, he will pass up food that looks or smells suspicious.

    Fortunately Redlegs' pups lived in a place where trapping
is forbidden. Even so, when the snow melted and the streams
once again began to flow, not all of them were present on
Miller Butte on their first birthday. Some of the older members
of the pack were missing, too. It is a sad fact that most wild
animals live short lives. For this reason they produce many
babies so no one species will die out.

And from all the signs that is exactly what Redlegs was about to do. Even before the snows had completely melted, she and Gray Dog cleaned out her old burrow.
Then Redlegs began acting strangely and staying off by herself. Gray Dog and Redlegs' grown-up pups wisely left her in peace. Though they did not yet know it, they were about to become baby-sitters for a new litter of pups.

This would be one task they would really enjoy. In fact, spring would be a most happy time for all the coyotes. Already the weather was warming, and ground squirrels and mice were becoming easy to find. And after the birth of new pups, life on Miller Butte would become very interesting, indeed.

The Miller Butte pack responded to all these changes. At dusk they gathered in a high place and howled until the surrounding hills echoed their bright song. For miles around people could hear the coyote chorus and were cheered by it. The coyotes seemed to be saying, Winter is finally over.

Soon everything on earth will begin anew.

AUTHOR'S NOTE

Finding a den of wild coyote pups is a difficult task. My aim—to watch pups grow—presented an even greater challenge. Coyotes have been hunted and trapped so much that they have become extremely wary. They are especially secretive in spring when they are raising their young. At this time not only do they keep out of sight, but at the least sign of anything strange, a mother coyote will move her babies to a new den.

That is why, during my first spring in coyote country, when I did finally succeed in locating a den of pups, I did not dare move close enough to photograph them. Instead I watched them from afar through a powerful telescope.

It was during this first year of study that I made the exciting discovery that the wild coyotes who lived on Miller Butte all helped in the raising of a litter of pups born to a female I named Redlegs. Both adult males and adult females guarded and fed this litter. They also brought food to the mother coyote while she was nursing.

The following year I returned to Miller Butte (on the National Elk Refuge in Wyoming) in the hope of photographing the same remarkable social behavior. After much difficulty I succeeded in finding the same coyotes again, and as luck would have it, I found that Redlegs had given birth to another litter! This time, because I wanted to take pictures, I had to find a way to be much closer to the den. So I drove a van across the land, almost up to the burrow. Then I hid in the van's windowless back and hoped that the coyotes would get used to it and believe it was empty. (I had brought along enough food to last me several weeks.)

But, to my disappointment, as soon as it grew dark the coyotes moved the pups. When I located them again, I repeated the same trick. I drove into position, then hid in the back of the truck. This time, although the animals acted suspicious of the apparently unoccupied vehicle, they did not move the pups.

Over the next few weeks I lived a quiet and solitary life. I took care not to make noise or be seen. I ate only uncooked food so that I wouldn't create unnecessary odors or smoke. When it grew dark, I crawled into my sleeping bag and went to sleep. But during the day I quietly recorded the comings and goings of the coyote family through my long camera lens poked through a curtained door.

Winter presented different problems for me, as well as for the coyotes. During this harsh season, coyotes must wander far and wide in search of food. Had I remained in one place, I very likely would not have seen any coyotes. So with the use of snowshoes and skis I traveled many miles across fields of snow, taking care to remain downwind and behind cover whenever possible. Sometimes I was lucky and came upon a coyote who was so intent on obtaining food that he did not immediately notice me behind a snowdrift or fir tree. When the camera shutter clicked, however, the animals would flee. Then I would have to begin my search anew.

That is how, little by little, I obtained pictures of the wild coyotes shown in this book.

— *Hope Ryden*